125 list!   80

MARTHA GRAHAM

Martha Graham

SIXTEEN DANCES IN PHOTOGRAPHS

by

BARBARA MORGAN

MORGAN & MORGAN • DOBBS FERRY, NEW YORK

Originally published under the same title, Martha Graham: Sixteen Dances in Photographs
by Duell, Sloan & Pearce in 1941
International Standard Book Number 0-87100-176-4
Library of Congress Catalog Card Number 80-81766
Printed in the United States of America by Morgan Press, Incorporated
145 Palisade Street, Dobbs Ferry, New York
All rights reserved in all countries.
No part of this book may be translated or reproduced or used in any form or by any means whatsoever
without permission in writing from the publisher.

*This book is a facsimile of the 1941 edition with the exception of an updated
choreographic record and the statements by Martha Graham and Barbara Morgan on pages 8 and 9.*

Copyright © 1941, 1980 by Barbara Morgan

First Revised Edition
Second Printing

Book design by Barbara Morgan

Morgan & Morgan, Inc.
Publishers
145 Palisade Street
Dobbs Ferry, New York 10522

To my husband

WILLARD D. MORGAN

ACKNOWLEDGMENT

and warmest thanks for collaboration extraordinary to ALL THE DANCERS.

to LOUIS HORST *for general counsel.*

to FRANCIS HAWKINS *for assistance with program material.*

to DR. RUSSELL POTTER *and* MARSHALL BROOKS *for theatre facilities.*

to ANN MEUER *for faithful photographic assistance.*

to ELIZABETH McCAUSLAND *for helpful text criticism.*

to RALPH GILBERT *for piano accompaniment.*

ACKNOWLEDGMENT — 1980

with gratitude and deep appreciation:

to MARTHA HILL

to DOUGLAS MORGAN

to LLOYD MORGAN

to LINDA HONGACH

to CECILIA YOUNCE

to LINDA HODGMAN

to LEONIDAS HERNANDEZ

to RONALD PROTAS

to CYNTHIA PARKER

to ROBERT GILL

CONTENTS

1980 PERSPECTIVES

It is rare that even an inspired photographer possesses the demonic eye which can capture the instant of a dance and transform it into a timeless gesture. In Barbara Morgan I found this person. In looking at these photographs today, I feel, as I felt when I first saw them, priviliged to have been a part of this collaboration. For to me, Barbara Morgan through her art reveals the inner landscape that is a dancer's world.

MARTHA GRAHAM
1980

SEEING Martha Graham dance in 1935 struck the same chord in me as seeing the Southwest Indian ritual dances. There on the desert with the distant mountains, the Indians conveyed a cosmic synthesis rhythmically unifying the People with the Sun, the Earth, and the fertility of all life.

So it is with Martha Graham's dances, which evoke spiritual-emotional energy. The inner core of Martha's art is her deep understanding of both the universal and the timeless; the uniquely individual and the common denominator of us all: the joys and sorrows, the hopes and fears, and the creative potentials of life.

I am grateful through photography to have been able to convey the spiritual vitality that emanates from the dances of Martha Graham.

BARBARA MORGAN
1980

DANCER'S FOCUS

I feel that I am indeed fortunate to have this book of photographs present a part of the work I have done. I like to think that it represents what is seen on the stage. What I may add in the way of words is in no way an explanation of the dances but is to be considered as a dancer's attitude toward the art in which she works.

THE only record of a dancer's art lies in the other arts. A dancer's instrument is his body bounded by birth and death. When he perishes his art perishes also. The art of dance is not arrested, but the world has only a legend about the individual, and the quality that has made him an artist. The work of an individual can be explained, criticized, or eulogized by means of the written word. A painting or a work of sculpture can give the world another artist's concept of a dancer. Photographs present more tangible evidence of a dancer's career. Photographs, when true to the laws that govern inspired photography, reveal facts of feature, bodily contour, and some secret of his power.

Every true dancer has a peculiar arrest of movement, an intensity of attention which animates his whole being. It may be called Spirit, or Dramatic Intensity, or Imagination, any word that explains why he does what he does. There is a sweeping line of intent that *services* his entire body. It is very like the act of listening. There is a complete focus upon a given instant.

I know of no other word for this dynamic except *co-ordination.* To me co-ordination means dominion of Spirit-of-body over all parts of the body, until it produces the unity that is passion. It is the activity produced by this Spirit-of-body that is Dancing. It is the organization of this activity that is the art that is Dance.

William Blake says: ''Execution is the chariot of genius.'' The art of the dance exists in the instant of execution. A dancer's life is focused on this instant of execution. This is not arrived at by thought, or desire, or wealth of idea only. It is all of these and more. It is acquired by formalized activity. Behind one perfect free leap are hundreds of leaps taken over a period of years. It is not more strange that freedom should be acquired by discipline than that spontaneity, that most natural-seeming of all moods, is not chance or happy accident, but is selected circumstance achieved by intention and design.

Dance is an absolute. It is not knowledge about something, but is knowledge itself. In that sense it is like music. It is independent of service to an idea, but is of such highly organized activity that it can produce idea. I am certain that movement never lies. The inner quality of the dancer is inherent in all that he does. I am not saying that a good person makes a good dancer or that a bad person makes a bad dancer. The motivation, the cause of the movement, establishes a center of gravity. This center of gravity induces the co-ordination that is body-spirit, and this Spirit-of-body is the state of innocence that is the secret of the absolute dancer. Gordon Craig makes two observation about dancing: ''Affectation appears only when the soul (vis motrix, motor force) is situated in any other point than the center of gravity.'' The other: ''Therefore, we must eat of the Tree of Knowledge in order to gain the state of innocence.''

Martha Graham

INTRODUCTION

My desire to make photographs of Martha Graham's dances originated in an exhibition in memory of Isadora Duncan. Among the photographs, drawings and sculpture, I saw only fragments of her greatness. Where was the Isadora we have from legend, who changed the history of dance and the history of human freedom? How did she move? What was the structure of her dance? We owe to Genthe, Steichen, Rodin, de Segonzac and Walkowitz illuminating glimpses of her, but more often these glimpses are of the great woman—not the great dancer. I was shocked to think that the work of any life can be so casually lost. I realized that we have lost the best of Isadora, Nijinsky and Pavlova, but that we need not lose the great dancing of our time through lack of recording. Today the increased scope of photography makes possible the fuller portrayal of the dancer's fugitive art.

At that time I had never photographed Martha Graham. I had never seen her except from a balcony seat, but I felt that her work had the revolutionary importance for us today that Duncan's had for yesterday. Isadora Duncan broke with academic formalism to express through her dance a richer human content in the democratic spirit of Walt Whitman. Martha Graham, carrying on this tradition, has found her own original expression for our complex new age.

Though the impulse to make this book came from the experience of a few hours, the work has taken more than four years to complete. The first pictures were taken at a New York Guild Theater rehearsal in 1936. Interruptions and changes have been numerous. Tours and rehearsals have interfered as well as the lack of theater backgrounds and photographic equipment. The delay, however, has had its compensations. During these years Graham has composed *Deep Song, American Document, Every Soul is a Circus, El Penitente* and *Letter to the World;* dances which have enriched her repertory, and greatly added to her significance. I, likewise, have had time to incorporate photographic experiment with a growing understanding of the essence of the dance.

In order to convey the meaning and the form of each dance, I have worked for pictures which contain the essential emotion of that dance. Such work is a kind of translation. The picture-page relationships serve as a bridge between the two mediums: Dancing and Photography. They communicate to the seeing reader the intense reality of movement contained in the original dance. My pictures are designed to arrest time and to capture the dance at its visual peak. Using still pictures, it is impossible to convey the emotion of thematic motion in literal sequence. The dance photograph must therefore select the most pregnant moments, and for emphasis make photographic use of lighting, scale and perspective. Yet it must not exaggerate or betray the spirit of the dance in the interests of sensational photography.

In making this book, I experimented with layouts that would suggest the dramatic sequence of the dances. This was a problem because of the subtle character of Martha Graham's art. She is herself the embodiment of the emotions she wants her audience to share. The emotional residue from her exciting, poignant movement has a strong hold on the memory. When Martha dances, she identifies herself so completely with her theme that we share her identification; our awareness is stretched.

The range of her conceptions may be read in the photographic shorthand of this book. In *Frontier* and *American Document* there is her love of democracy. In *Letter to the World* and *Every Soul is a Circus* there is compassionate humor, fantasy, and romance. *Deep Song* expresses her sympathy for all who struggle for liberty. *Celebration, Ekstasis, Primitive Mysteries* and *Lamentation* contain the universal joy, sorrow, and mystery of life.

The sixteen dances shown in these photographs have been chosen by Martha Graham as her most important works. Louis Horst's "Choreographic Record" gives the complete list of her compositions. The repertory brings us to 1941; but as the book goes to press, Graham has several new dances in preparation. Her desire for perfection leads her to revise the existing dances continually; so do not be surprised if the decor of *Every Soul is a Circus* changes spots in mid-book. Also there have been changes in the personnel of the dance company during this time, notably the addition of her partner, Erick Hawkins, and other male dancers who have made possible a more complete range of emotion.

The text has been contributed by Martha Graham herself, by Louis Horst, her musical director, and by George Beiswanger, assistant editor of Theatre Arts Monthly in charge of its dance department. For eleven years Mr. Horst was musical director for Ruth St. Denis. Ever since Martha Graham has given her own concerts Mr. Horst has been her musical director, frequently her composer, and always her helpful critic. Mr. Beiswanger, writing as one who has followed Miss Graham's work over many years of its development, draws relationship between forces of her life and the shape of her art.

I present these photographs for the pleasure of those who know Martha Graham's work; as a source work for dancers, critics and historians. More than that I present them for all people who care for the dance; and who find in these images something of man's struggle for freedom.

BARBARA MORGAN

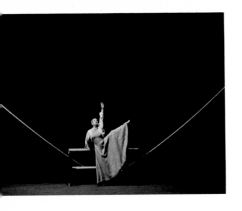

FRONTIER

Frontier, subtitled "American Perspective of the Plains," is a tribute to the vision, and independence of the pioneer woman. It portrays her strength, and tenderness, her determination and jubilation at overcoming the hazards of a new land, as well as her love for the land. The movement, completely one with the decor's widening horizon, evokes the feeling of distance, loneliness and courage. *Frontier* is an American classic. It is as closely identified with Martha Graham as the "Swan Dance" was with Pavlova.

Choreography and costume . . . . *Martha Graham*
Music . . . . *Louis Horst*   *Decor* . . . . *Isamu Noguchi*

LAMENTATION

Lamentation is a "dance of sorrows." It is not the sorrow of specific person, time or place, but the personification of grief itself.

Choreography and costume . . . . *Martha Graham*   *Music* . . . . *Zoltan Kodaly*

EKSTASIS

Ekstasis reveals the exquisite awareness of the body in motion: shifting balances, alternating tensions, delight issuing from inevitabilities.

Choreography and costume . . . . *Martha Graham*   *Music* . . . . *Lehman Engle*

CELEBRATION

Celebration expresses the intense inner excitement we feel in the face of great events. Its rhythms, fast and furious and soft and lyrical by turn, portray the spirit's triumph.

Choreography and costume . . . . *Martha Graham*   *Music* . . . . *Louis Horst*

PRIMITIVE MYSTERIES

Primitive Mysteries, in three parts: "Hymn to the Virgin," "Crucifixus" and "Hosanna." It derives its style from that strange, beautiful unity born of the meeting of Spanish Christianity and the native religion of the Indian Southwest. The dance is written in terms of childlike simplicity. Economical in movement, it is exalted and gentle in mood. Martha Graham, in a white costume, suggests the statues of the Virgin in the adobe churches of the Southwest and Mexico. The Dance Group in dark blue costumes forms the background and acts as a chorus to the solo dancer's joy in the "Hymn to the Virgin," to her tragic grief in "Crucifixus," and to her exaltation in "Hosanna."

Choreography and costume . . . . *Martha Graham*   *Music* . . . . *Louis Horst*

DANCES IN PHOTOGRAPHS

AMERICAN PROVINCIALS
I. Act of Piety   II. Act of Judgment

American Provincials has as its background the world of Hawthorne's Scarlet Letter. "A mighty and terrifying holiness is invoked with heroic frenzy. Departure on the part of one from tradition results in a ferocious condemnation, part sex, part pride, all demoniacal."

John Martin, New York Times

Choreography . . . . *Martha Graham*
Music . . . . *Louis Horst* *Costumes* . . . . *Martha Graham*

HARLEQUINADE
Pessimist
Optimist

Harlequinade, woeful and joyful, is subtly ironic. The Pessimist turns little woes into mountainous sorrows and weeps inconsolably into a large polka dot handkerchief and in the end converts this receptacle for tears into an empty but crushingly heavy pack, slung over the shoulder. The Optimist ties the same polka dot kerchief at waist and reels with laughter at the cares the Pessimist wept for.

Choreography and costume . . . . *Martha Graham* *Music* . . . . *Ernest Toch*

IMPERIAL GESTURE

A dance of arrogance and sychophancy. Its animated symbol is a great stiff skirt.

Choregraphy and costume . . . . *Martha Graham* *Music* . . . . *Lehman Engel*

SARABANDE

An old court dance title is used sardonically in this dance. The action exaggerates ceremonious behavior, using as its thematic movement the curtsey.

Choreography and costume . . . . *Martha Graham* *Music* . . . . *Lehman Engel*

PRIMITIVE CANTICLES

Ave
Salve

Here religous possession is characterized by alternating calm faith and ecstatic frenzy.

Choreography and costume .... *Martha Graham*   *Music* .... *Villa-Lobos*

DEEP SONG

Deep Song was created at the beginning of the War in Spain. The forms of the dance—its swirls, crawls on the floor, contractions and falls—are kinetic equivalents of the human experience in war which inspired *Deep Song.* It is the anatomy of anguish from tragic events.

Choreography .... *Martha Graham*
Music .... *Henry Cowell*   *Costume* .... *Martha Graham*

SATYRIC FESTIVAL SONG

Satyric Festival Song has the irreverent bold charm of a satyr's laugh. It mocks pomposity like a clown, poking fun with rude gestures and attitudes.

Choreography and costume .... *Martha Graham*   *Music* .... *Imre Weisshaus*

EL PENITENTE

The Penitentes of the Southwest are a sect which believes in purification from sin through severe penance. Even today, in Old and New Mexico, they practice ancient rites, including the crucifixion. The dance bears no factual relationship to these practices but is presented as a story told after the manner of the old mystery plays. The three figures enter, assume their characters and perform as a group of players. The festival dance at the end is a version of popular dance of celebration with no ritualistic content.

Choreography .... *Martha Graham*
Music .... *Louis Horst*   *Costumes* .... *Martha Graham*

EVERY SOUL IS A CIRCUS • A Satire

This is not the literal circus of canvas and sawdust ring, but a circus of ridiculous situations and silly behaviors. In every woman there is a desire to be featured in a "star turn," as the apex of a triangle and as the beloved of a duet. In the life of every woman there is some force which, however temporarily, holds the whip hand. Throughout the circus of her life every woman is her own most appreciative spectator. In this circus of the silly woman's life, the sum total of episodes and of interludes does not add up to mature dignity but to tragic, addled confusion.

Choreography	Martha Graham	Music	Paul Nordoff
Costumes	Edythe Gilfond	Decor	Phillip Stapp

Thanks are due Macmillan for permission to quote from Vachel Lindsay's poem "Every Soul is a Circus."

LETTER TO THE WORLD

The title of *Letter to the World* is a line from a poem by Emily Dickinson, and all the spoken words are from her poems. The action is built on the legend of her life. The scene is laid in the shadow world of her imagination as set forth in her poems, rather than in the real world of Amherst where she lived. No one character in *Letter to the World* is meant to portray Emily Dickinson: each character is some one aspect of her personality. "The Children," "The Fairy Queen," and the "Young Girl" are extensions of herself in childhood, adolescence and young womanhood. The "Ancestress" is the embodiment of her background—Puritan, awesome, beautiful—and the symbol of the death-fear constantly in her mind. "March" and the other men are extensions of the "Lover" who in turn represent Emily's gesture toward happiness. The loss of her lover forces her to face her destiny as a poet with the realization that her happiness must be found in the intensity of her work.

Choreography	Martha Graham	Music	Hunter Johnson
Costumes	Edythe Gilfond	Decor	Arch Lauterer

Thanks are due Little Brown and Co. for permission to quote from the poems of Emily Dickinson for "Letter To The World."

AMERICAN DOCUMENT

"Our documents are our legends—our poignantly near history, our folk tales." American Document stems from our national background. Its form is built loosely on the minstrel show which is closely identified with American life and drama. Action opens with the "walk around," a parade of characters. A repetition of this "walk around" serves to divide the episodes throughout the piece, as the curtain does in theatre. The work is dramatic but not drama. Essentially documentary, American Document progresses from the Indian Episode to the Puritan, through the Emancipation period to the present. Words are spoken on the stage by an interlocutor to bring into focus the action of the dance. The lines spoken by the interlocutor are from the Declaration of Independence, a letter from Red Jacket of the Senecas, Lincoln's Gettysburg Address, Jonathon Edwards' sermons, the Song of Songs, Walt Whitman's poems and other important American letters. American Document is an adventure in theatre made necessary by the broad scope of the choreographer's idea.

Choreography			Martha Graham
Music	Ray Green	Costumes	Martha Graham

FRONTIER

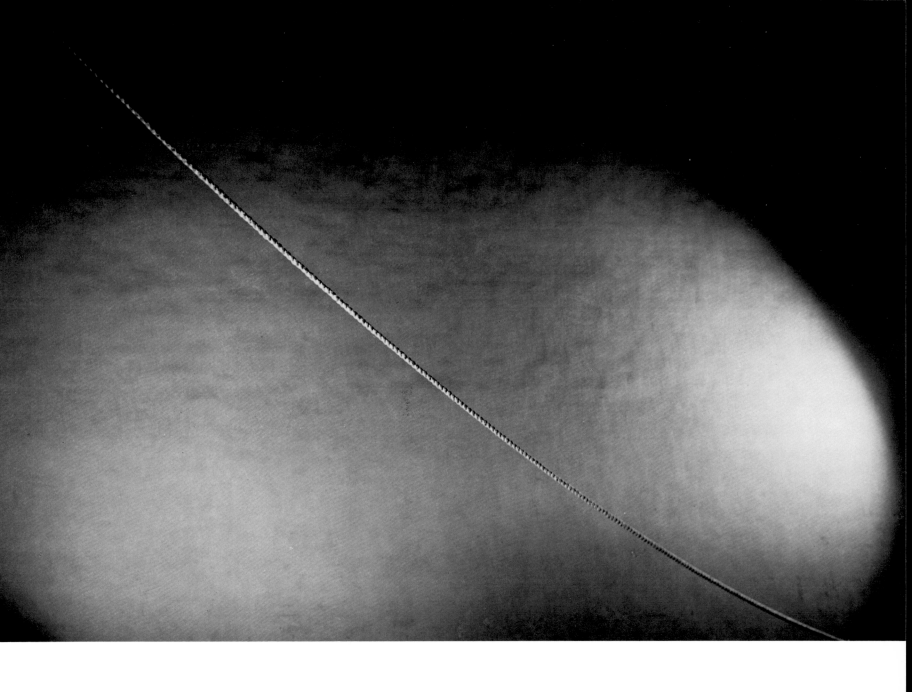

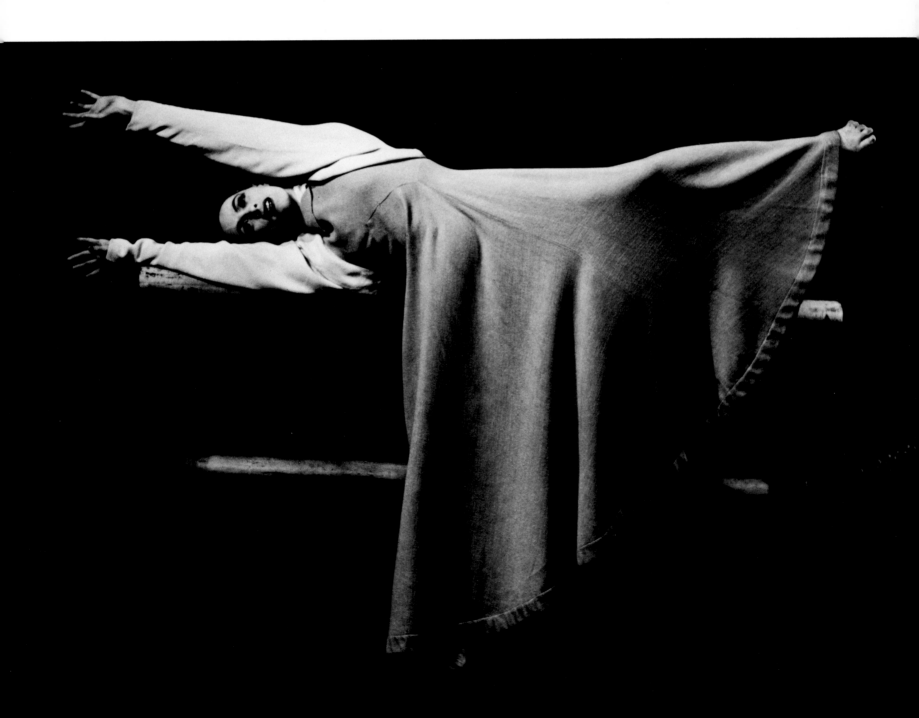

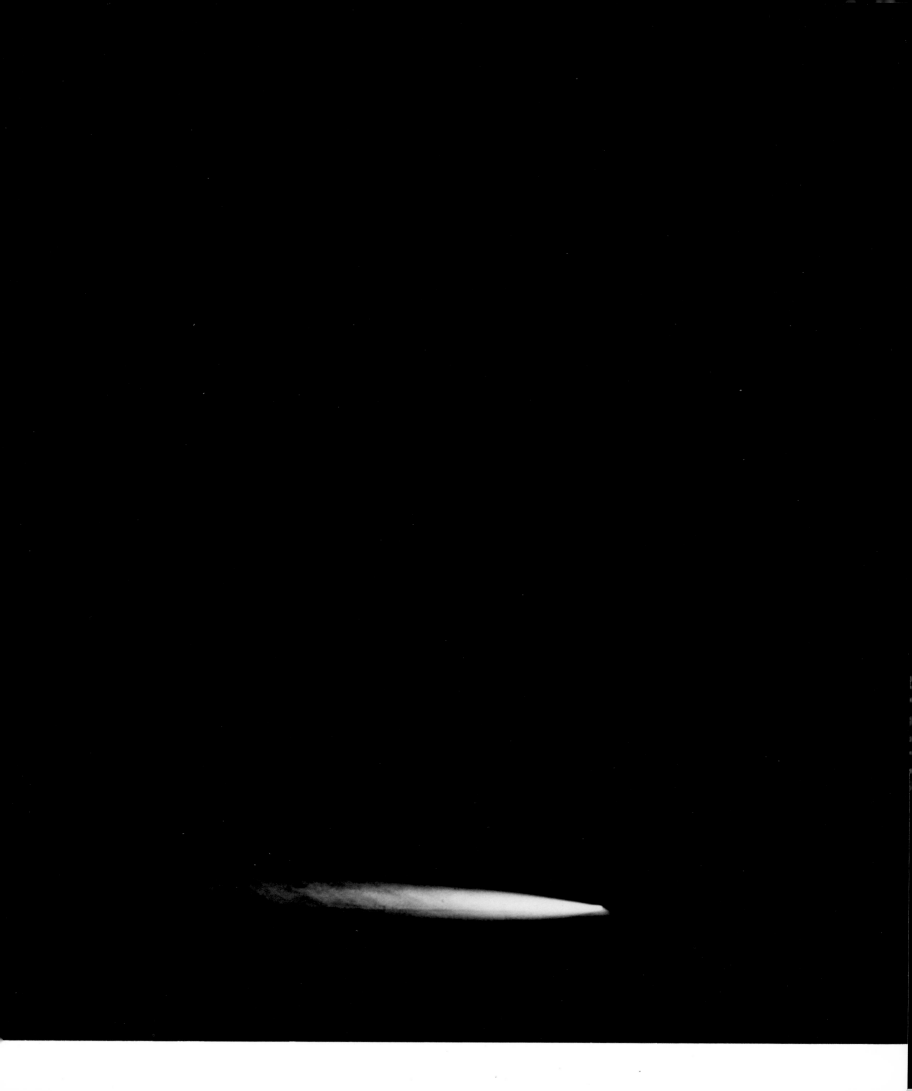

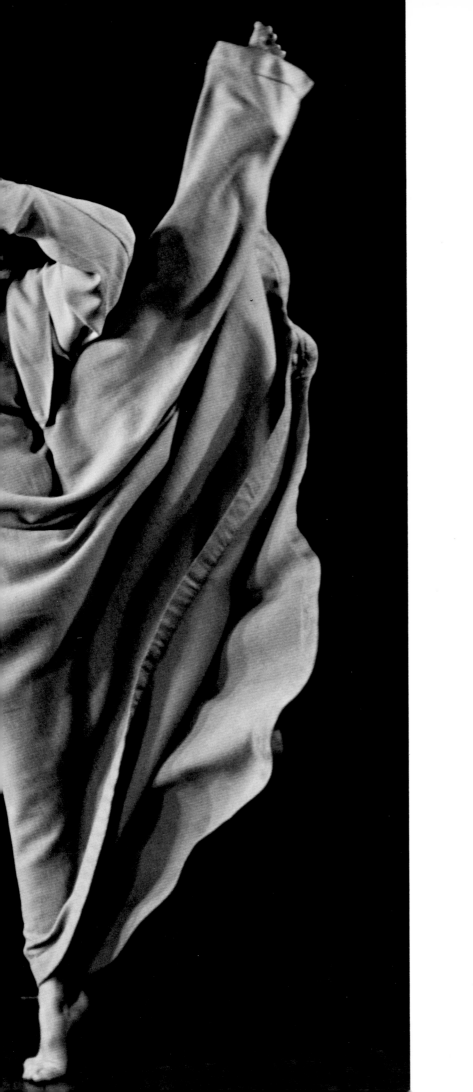

LAMENTATION

EKSTASIS

CELEBRATION

PRIMITIVE MYSTERIES

Hymn to the Virgin

Crucifixus

Hosanna

AMERICAN PROVINCIALS

Act of Piety
Act of Judgment

IMPERIAL GESTURE

SARABANDE

PRIMITIVE CANTICLES

SALVE

DEEP SONG

SATYRIC FESTIVAL SONG

EL PENITENTE

CHARACTERS:

Penitent	.... Erick Hawkins
Christ Figure	.... Merce Cunningham
Mary Figure	
Virgin	
Magdalen	.... Martha Graham
Mother	

ACTION:

1. Entrance of Performers
2. Flagellation of Penitent
3. Vision of Penitent
      The Virgin Pleads
      The Christ Blesses
4. Seduction
      The Magdalen seduces the Penitent
5. Death Cart
      The Death Cart is the symbol for sin
6. Fall of Man
7. Christ condemns
8. The Penitent bears the cross on his back
9. Crucifixion
      The Penitent atones and wins salvation
10. Festival Dance

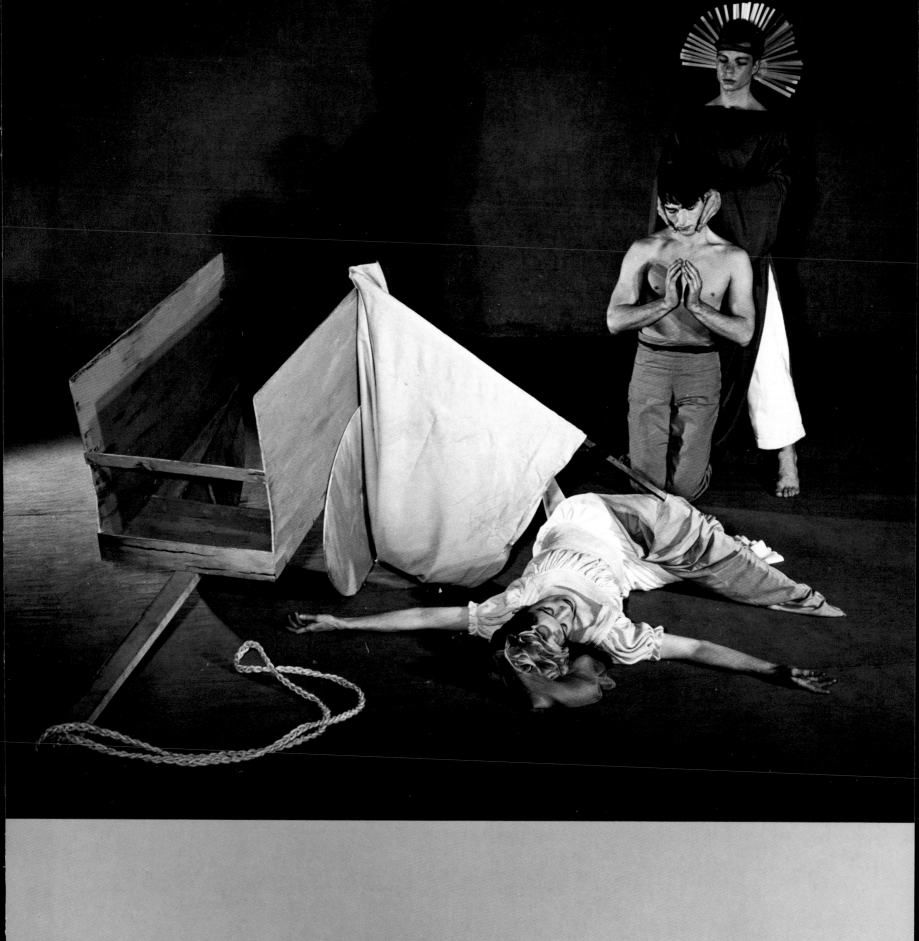

CHARACTERS OF THE ARENIC WORLD

Empress of the Arena . . . . Martha Graham

Ring Master . . . . Erick Hawkins

Acrobat . . . . Merce Cunningham

Ideal Spectator . . . . Jean Erdman

First Arenic Performer . . . . Nelle Fisher

Other Arenic Performers: Sophie Maslow, Ethel Butler, Frieda Flier, Marjorie Mazia

EVERY SOUL IS A CIRCUS

EMPRESS OF THE ARENA

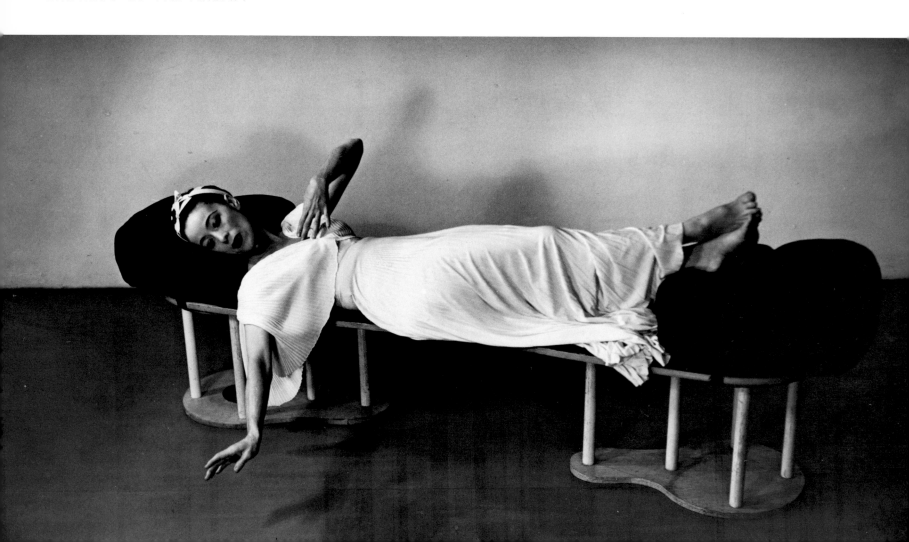

RINGMASTER

STAR TURN

GARLAND
ENTRY

ARENIC WORLD TRIANGLE

"POSES AND PLASTIQUES"

"Every soul is a Circus
Every mind is a tent
Every heart is a sawdust ring
Where the circling race is spent."

LETTER TO THE WORLD

"I'm nobody! Who are you?

Are you nobody, too?
Then there's a pair of us."

CHARACTERS:

One Who Dances . . . . Martha Graham

One Who Speaks . . . . Jean Erdman

Lover . . . . Erick Hawkins

Ancestress . . . . Jane Dudley

March . . . . Merce Cunningham

Young Girl . . . . Sophie Maslow

Fairy Queen . . . . Frieda Flier

Two Children . . . . . . Nina Fonaroff, Marjorie Maszia

and
Ethel Butler, Elizabeth Halpern, David Campbell,
David Zellmer, Sascha Liebich

"'Tis Conscience, childhood's nurse."

ACTION:

1. "Because I see New Englandly"
        "Life is a spell"
        Party

2. "The Postponeless Creature"
        Ancestress
        "Gay Ghastly Holiday"

3. "The Little Tippler"
        "Dear March, come in!"
        The Fairy Queen
        The picnic

4. "Leaf at love turned back"

5. Letter

"Let us play yesterday—
I the girl at school,
You and Eternity
The untold tale."

THE PARTY

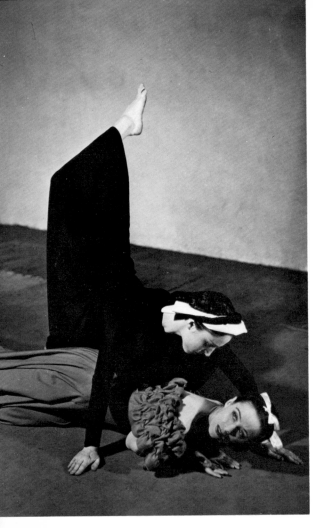

"It's coming — the postponeless Creature"

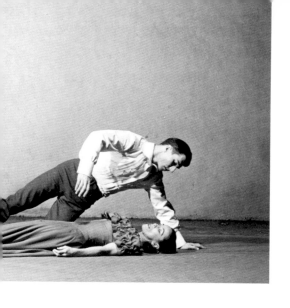

"Gay, ghastly holiday!"

"I'm saying every day
'If I should be a Queen tomorrow
I'd do this way.'"

"DEAR MARCH, COME IN!"

"Lightly stepped a yellow star
To its lofty place,
Loosed the Moon her silver hat
From her lustral face.
All of evening softly lit
As an astral hall —
'Father,' I observed to Heaven,
'You are Punctual.' "

"I'm wife; I've finished that,
That other state;

How odd the girl's life looks
Behind this soft eclipse!

But why compare?
I'm wife! Stop there!"

"AND CARRIES ONE OUT TO GOD."

"Of course I prayed —
And did God care?
He cared as much
As on the air
A bird had stamped her foot
And cried 'Give me!' "

"This is my letter to the world"

AMERICAN DOCUMENT

AMERICAN DOCUMENT

The place is here in the United States of America . . . . . . The time is now:

DECLARATION   "We hold these truths to be self-evident:

That all men are created equal"

INDIAN
EPISODE

"I do not remember the flocks of pigeons in the virgin forest,

"LISTEN TO WHAT WE SAY:

There was a time when our forefathers owned this great island . . .
Their seats extended from the rising to the setting sun."

Before these states were   .   .   .   .   .   but my blood remembers   .   .   .   .   .   my heart remembers."

PURITAN
EPISODE

A stiff-necked generation claims the land,
Claims the Lord, denying the tender creature.

"I am my beloved's, and his desire is towards me."

EMANCIPATION
EPISODE

"All persons held as slaves shall be then, thenceforward and forever free."

NOW   This is one man . . . .

this is one million men . . . .

This man has a power. It is himself, and you. . . . .

We are three women . . . . we are three million women. . . . .

We are the mothers of the hungry dead . . . . . We are the mothers of the hungry living.

AMERICAN DOCUMENT

"That Government of the people
by the people
and for the people
shall not perish from the earth."

MARTHA GRAHAM: A Perspective

George Beiswanger

In a paradoxical but very real sense, the artist *is* his works. They are his best explanation—the one clear and consummate exposition of his needs, his purposes, his being. They are what the artist lives for—and what lives on after the personal story is finished. All the rest is material and background: the stuff of experience that is made into art; the background of incident and event that reflects the glory shed upon it by what the artist has created.

It tells us next to nothing, in and of itself, that Martha Graham is a tenth generation American of New England, New York Dutch, Scotch and Irish background; that she was born in a suburb of Pittsburgh of a doctor father and a mother descended in straight line from Miles Standish; that she staged spontaneous bits of drama-dance as a child; that she did not see a dance concert until she was thirteen; that it was with some persuasion that her father finally consented to her enrollment in the Denishawn School in Los Angeles. All this might be the story of any number of young girls who have danced for a while and then turned to other pursuits.

Perhaps it is more significant that shortly she was teaching as well as studying at Denishawn, that she soon became a featured dancer of the company on tour, and that in 1923 John Murray Anderson saw enough in her to engage her for one, then a second edition of the Greenwich Village Follies. But to place one's finger upon the future artist, the artist whose lineage and background, childhood experience and apprentice years would later be given profound meaning by the dances into which they were wrought, one must seek out the person who left Denishawn because she found little in its method and repertory to nourish her own inner being; who nevertheless took with her a firmly established sense of theatre and an abiding conception of dance as a way of life. But this person—Martha Graham would have said—did not yet exist: except as a bundle of needs and drives. It was a person struggling to be born—from the moment when she began to teach, to dance, and to work with a group of her own at the Eastman School of Music until the day came when she could say, "To me what I am doing is natural. It fits me as my skin fits me."

The story, then, of the early years of Martha Graham's career is one of continuous, agonized search within; and without—a sturdy and defiant declaration of the right to search. What New York City saw at the programs of 1926, 1927, 1928 and 1929 was a dance talent undeniably of the first water; a taut and apparently wilful revolutionary; a language and a stage presence that repelled as often as it attracted; the first bold, as yet unjoined timbers of a new form and style in dancing; and the indefinable but unmistakable aura of dance magic—that emanation of power to which, for want of a better term, we give the name genius. All this in programs that were part vestigial, part tentative and part downright floundering.

"The first young stages of an artist have no freshness; they have only a fresh feeling, or egotism or exhibitionism that is but partially expressed in form that is either casual or traditional or imitative," so wrote Stark Young with these early years in mind. The surprising thing, as he also remarked, is that the young artist knew this—if not intellectually, then by the artist-mind that was working its way through the thickets with indomitable energy and a fairly ruthless integrity. "Her method of pressing forward," Edith J. R. Isaacs observed, "is by dancing through a problem first, and thinking through it afterward."

What were the problems? For one, to rid herself of what she did not need and could not use. Martha Graham herself has said that an artist has "to destroy himself" in order to create. It was not merely a matter of sloughing off this manner and that technique. A whole self had to be danced out and away: the easy beauty pilloried in *Deux Valses Sentimentales* (1926); the romantic woman mirrored in *Fragilité* (1927); the venerable dance pretenses—petulance, remorse, politeness and vivacity—dissected in *Four Insincerities* (1929). It is characteristic that the artist saw these not just as modes of dance to be caricatured but as demons to be exorcised. Her weapon was satire, and would later have added to it the sword of denunciation; but already she had found a basic theme, the strength and tenacity of spurious emotions in the web of human experience.

Companion to this act of "destruction" was the effort to lay bare the impulses from which the affirmative stuff of art spring. They had to be dug out and acknowledged before they could be expresssed. *Desir* (1926) was the first dance to come out of an "inner compulsion" of this sort. *Adolescence* (1929) welled up from the same source. But dances on this order were to be few and far between during these first years; the lyric note would seldom be sounded. The problem was personal, of course. Every artist knows how resistant the wall is between passion and expression, how little he knows what it really is he wants to say, and how difficult it is to say it with truth. Thomas Wolfe has recorded the story for all time in his novels. But the problem was set in a larger framework. Dance had long forgotten that "the affirmation of life through movement"—to use Martha Graham's own words—was its chief task. Furthermore, the desire to draw from deep wells was largely inhibited in the American character itself, so far as conscious art-making was concerned.

To make any headway, it was necessary to build a new body, or more accurately, to restore the "natural" body so that it could once again dance with freedom and power. "Movement in the modern dance is the product not of invention but of discovery—discovery of what the body will do, and what it can do in the expression of emotion... It takes ten years to build a dancer." The first sentence and its stern corollary were wrung from experience. Martha Graham had to learn the language and structure of dance for herself; she was not taught, and—given the age and its cultural state—there was little she could have been taught. With her as with Cezanne and Van Gogh, Picasso and Matisse—whose paintings she studied and whose writings she read—the surface of dance (the conventional idioms, the accepted evasions, the brittle shell) had to be "broken up," so that the underlying structure could be disclosed. With the modern composers—whose music was fed to her by her musical director, Louis Horst, as soon as it was published or could be obtained in manuscript form—she searched for a beat, a rhythm that would release feeling and the will to form. Like all beginnings, the new style came in fragments at first—here a bit of technique, there a pattern, yonder a basic insight. First principles are bare. The rich, the round, the full would come later.

Finally, the young dancer had to become aware of the kind of world in which she was living. It was an urban world—the big city of the twenties with its inequalities, its cruelties, its brash self-satisfaction. Martha Graham had grown up in Santa Barbara where the country, the climate and a middle-class home combined to shield her from the harsher realities. New York City tore off the veil, as it has done for so many American artists and writers. The first dance to reflect this awakened social consciousness was *Revolt* (1927). *Immigrant* and *Poems of 1917* followed in 1928. The tongue of protest was unloosed and a thoroughly indigenous American voice spoke out—to be itself branded for a while as "radical," to have its own ironical innings with the "professionals" in that field, but finally to be listened to for what Lincoln Kirstein has called the "candid, sweeping and wind-worn liberty" of its expression.

Nothing from these years was to remain in the repertory for long. The artist had been "building soil," planting seed, tending the early, tentative shoots, testing and cutting away the unfruitful. But with *Heretic* (1929) the harvest was at hand—a first period of large work which brought *Lamentation* and *Harlequinade* (1930), *Primitive Canticles* and

Primitive Mysteries (1931), *Sarabande* and *Celebration* (1934)—to mention only the dances pictured in this book.

The fruitage was along three lines: the appearance of the mature "Graham" solo dance; the emergence of a definitive group style; the mastery of the suite form. As to the first, Edward Schloss supplied the significant clue when he wrote of *Lamentation*, "Martha Graham does not depict grief; she *is* grief." This effect—communicated in every one of her solos whether by itself or in group composition—is no accident, the mere result of technical virtuosity and a superb theatre presence. It is the inevitable outcome—to quote John Martin —of "a purpose to pierce through all the strata of the trivial to the roots of human experience." It is the product of an imaginative capacity to extract the emotional core of a character and its key trait, to create out of that core an archetypal figure which becomes its embodiment, and to discover those "first movements"—to use Isadora Duncan's pregnant phrase—which disclose the soul thus bared. The bereft, enduring "mothers" of *Lamentation, Immediate Tragedy* and *Deep Song;* the Saint Joan of *Heretic;* the figures of incarnate violence and pride in *Act of Piety, Sarabande* and *Imperial Gesture;* the Virgin Mother in *Canticles* and *Mysteries;* even the goat creature of *Satyric Festival*, the "silly woman" of *Circus* and the Emily Dickinson of *Letter*—these are mythic beings, "ancestral shapes," independent of space and time. "We are three women; we are three million women...I am one man; I am one million men." The words are from *Document*, but they might be the signature of every being that inhabits the lofty world of Martha Graham's imagination.

In every case, these enlarged beings draw virtue and strength from a Dionysiac joy in movement, the "strong, free, joyous action" of which Nietzsche wrote. From the same source came Martha Graham's way with the group. There is neither need nor space to speak here of the technical base: the development in each member of the group of an integrated dance person; the insistence upon precision, virtuosity and fire; the perfecting of an ensemble that danced as one body and one will. *Celebration* was a succinct and splendid exposition of these, "the stuff" of dance. Beyond this, what the period brought was the authoritative use of the group as a dramatic force. It became the implacable wall against which the heretic beat, the bar of judgment before which the arrogant are brought, the devout by whom and in whom the sacred mysteries are wrought. One thinks of the Greek chorus, but with a difference. The Graham group does not comment; it acts. It takes fate into its own hands; often it *is* fate. Its dancers are the "inspired damsels" of *The Bacchae;* Euripides would have understood.

Given protagonist and group, given the myth of eternal warfare between life and death which runs through Martha Graham's work, given also the austerity with which the battle was envisioned at this stage in her dancing, the suite form was inevitable. Dance movements, each a compact drama in itself—were tied together by a theme, combined in a sequence of ideas. The unity was not so much dramatic as a matter of over-all mood and style—a style so sure of itself at its height and so exalted that it left the spectator in breathless, reverent amazement. It was of *Primitive Mysteries* that Stark Young wrote: ''I can say that it is one of the few things I have ever seen in dancing where the idea, its origin, the source from which it grew, the development of its excitement and sanctity, give me a sense of baffled awe and surprise, the sense of wonder and defeat in its beautiful presence.'' One may add that while composing it Martha Graham steeped herself in Bach's B minor Mass; but that does not explain the final wonder of its impress.

Throughout these years, good and evil remained juxtaposed but unresolved: arrogance and fortitude; hypocrisy and piety; frustration and freedom; the tragedy and the comedy of life. Indignation and irony—while at moments sheer Irish mischief peeped through—these are the defenses of the warring heart. They formed the surface of a dance whose substance was not always completely disclosed; and they were what the audience-at-large often considered pure Graham-esque. The judgment was unfair, but that is beside the point. For the artist was now ready to supply her own corrective—to begin a period of new growth that would lead eventually to her own ''letter to the world.'' The ultimate goal of this period was to be a tremendous one: to see in the tragedy, the defeat of life the reason for an undying affirmation of man's will to become truly human; to create a dance form capable of bearing the full weight of this insight.

The first step was the digging of deeper roots into native soil. Two otherwise fallow seasons brought *Frontier* (1935) and with it ''the American theme.'' In and of itself the phrase is misleading; Martha Graham had been dancing about America ever since she started. But it was an America that had fallen apart, forgotten its faiths, lost its sense of spiritual destiny. ''I may not remember, but my blood remembers,'' the Interlocutor says in *Document.* Martha Graham began to remember, not in order to escape but to bring to bear upon today's perplexities all that was sturdy and upright and liberating in the American dream. Listening over the radio to evil words spoken by men across the seas, she recalled other words—the Declaration of Independence, the Emancipation Proclamation, the poems of Walt Whitman, the Bible—that had once held power for good. *American Document* (1938) was the result. The affirmations toward which the artist had been feeling from *Panorama* (1935) to *American Lyric* (1937) at last came clear.

What was equally important, however, was the fact that the exciting framework of *Document* and the use of the speaking voice pointed the way toward a large and integrated dance form: a form that would bring to the new dance that which was valid in the traditional structure of the ballet, the motifs and thematic methods of sonata and symphony, and the essential stuff of the poetic drama. The works which now ensued—*Every Soul Is a Circus, El Penitente* and *Letter to the World*—pushed this form to immediate maturity. All things, as a matter of fact, had been converging toward this end: Martha Graham's own technique and style; the insistence that dance as an affirmative art force set its own patterns—music and decor to conform; the powerful impetus toward integration received as early as *Canticles* and *Mysteries* from the surviving Indian culture of the Southwest; the opportunities to work in the larger framework of the theatre which came from the days of the Neighborhood Playhouse and its dance-music dramas to the Cornell-McClintic production of *Romeo and Juliet* (1934) and Archibald MacLeish's *Panic* (1935).

But even more strategic was the realization on the part of the artist that it was no longer necessary to "take a stand," to make each new dance relentlessly subserve the affirmation of some significant and challenged truth. This release, which came first with *Circus*, this new feeling of the right to breathe art's own free air, meant the final emergence of the artist as a theatre person. At last one could speak without quibbling of "the theatre" of Martha Graham.

In this theatre there is story—the parable of everywoman when she happens to be a Madame Bovary; the pilgrim's progress of sinning, aspiring man; the legend of Emily Dickinson—poet. There is speech—dance evoked—that does for dance what sound has done for the film. Above all, there is tragedy and comedy, co-mingled as they are in life, resolved and reconciled in a soul which has won its battle and knows whereon it stands. Gaiety, tenderness, solemnity, mischief, love, despair, wilfulness, submission, piety, the questioning heart, dark hours, exaltation, the bitterness of death and the ecstasy of living—all have found a home together.

The dance-poet—the "maker"—stands complete. What dances are new to come cannot, of course, be foretold. No great artist is "predictable." But whatever they are, one thing is sure. They, too, will be the work of one to whom life has spoken face to face.

DANCE INTO PHOTOGRAPHY

Barbara Morgan

Every dance has peaks of emotional intensity; moments when the dance ''speaks'' to the audience. These are the moments when the form of the dance is in closest unison with the original compulsion which gave it birth. Dance is experienced continuously in time and space, but is remembered by these instants of combustion. While we are watching it, gestures and attitudes may seem unforgettable, but the crescendo of attention ends when the curtain goes down. The trivial dance ends when the performance is over, but the great dance haunts the memory. Why? Because a vital essence, projected most intensely in these peaks, stirs the memory again and again, although the merely transitional movements may fade away. It is the role of photography to seize such moments; to fuse reality, art and time.

Dance photography deals with definite moments of expressive action. But the six-and-a-half minute performance time of *Frontier* bears no relation to the timeless quality of excitement felt by the audience when the curtain rises. In this dance two diverging ropes extend to the horizon. There stands the small, courageous figure of the pioneer woman. She dances her vision of a home on the land—rejoicing in a sense of space and freedom. Then comes a feeling of insecurity and a premonition of disaster; but her faith and self-reliance come flooding back. Finally she reaffirms her belief in the American continent, and in courage equal to survival. The dance makes use of rhythmical time, subtly measured by the disciplined body, to free the imagination of the audience. The photographer, employing the fine precisions of lens-time, film-time, and nerve-time makes a bridge between clock-time and emotional-time.

Dance forms are fluid; they merge continually; and they pass so soon! The seemingly rhapsodic flow of the dance is actually a sequence of modulated motions. What are the significant moments for the photographer; and how are they to be chosen? I make my selection by watching a great many performances and rehearsals—noticing especially what is discarded. After absorbing as much as possible, I find that certain gestures remain vividly fixed in my memory, and come to symbolize the whole dance. I believe the images that I retain in this spontaneous way have reality; and it is these that I translate into photographic terms.

Since the dance is plastic and the photograph graphic, there is a problem of translation. How are these moments, whose medium is motion, to be expressed in the motionless photograph? There can be an exchange of values. For instance; tension in the photograph may evoke tension of the dance, nuance in the photograph, a nuance of the dance. But before he can hope to reveal the soul of the dance, the photographer must deal with complicated technical problems.

I have experimented with many types of cameras trying to gain all the essentials in this kind of work. Maximum speed, depth of field, ease of handling, reliable synchronization, and adequate negative size are all important. While no one camera can satisfy all demands, the one I have found most adaptable is the 4 × 5 Speed Graphic with which most of these pictures have been made.

Although I use regular photographic spotlights and floodlights for some subjects, I work chiefly with multiple flashlight, using a Kalart focal plane synchronizer and a special battery booster. The abundance of light stops action and allows the lens to be closed down to obtain sharpness of focus for the figures in different planes within the deep stage space. However, I do not believe in the fetish of sharp focus for sharpness' sake and I often throw a subordinate part of the design out of focus to emphasize the center of interest. With the exception of some solos, duets and trios, which were photographed in my studio, the pictures were taken in New York theaters, but not in official performance.

Lighting arrangements range between extremes according to the design—from a single flash bulb to illuminate an *American Provincials* solo in my studio, to a multiple flash hook-up of many lights to expose for fast action of the entire company, as in *American Document* and *Letter to the World*. In the latter case I perched on a tall ladder in the orchestra seats, while from my synchronized camera, wires carried fanwise to the stage and overhead, to the sides front and the sides rear, where assistants held them or mounted them on high standards as needed. This lighting method is so flexible that it does not wear down the élan of the dancer as badly as stage lighting with floods and spots. There is no heat from the flash, to make the dancers perspire and to spoil their make-up and tempers.

Second in importance to knowing what I want to picture is knowing how to foresee the design in terms of light, timing and spacing. When I work with spots and floods, I can move the lights around by trial and error until the effect is right, but in flash photography there is no margin for error. It will be entirely good or entirely bad. It must be visualized straight and true the first time, before placing the reflectors, adjusting their angle, and releasing the synchronized lights. Pilot lights are often used to see the design before flashing the bulbs; but I have discarded them as just one more gadget and instead have trained myself, before I press the shutter release, to evaluate mentally the interplay of light on the moving forms—as it creates shadows, and is being modified by counter lights and their shadows. I try to keep the picture unified with a dominant source of light, into which I may throw subordinate lights for sculptural modeling; lights to free the bodies in space, and lights and shadows for psychological overtones or architectural framing. Overhead lighting and back lighting are very important to free the figures in space. Like the carom of a billiard ball, I often send light from the side-rear to the back of the stage, thence to rebound at the dancers.

Lighting can never be thought of separately from timing. The form of a static subject is as it is: but the form of a moving subject is altered not only by its own changing shape but by the interpretation imparted by camera timing. At 1/500 second shutter speed of the camera, the *Frontier* costume billows; at 1/1000 second it would have lashed out, destroying that gentle buoyance registered at the slower speed. Timing should be attuned with musical precision to the character implicit in the action. Over-fast freezing of the action will always make a sensational picture but it may reveal body tensions psychologically foreign to the intention of the dance. In a centrifugal whirl, the body center is moving more slowly than the finger-tips and the costume at the periphery. Timing determines whether the over-all action is to be frozen or whether the sense of motion will be increased by blurring movement. In the latter case the shutter speed must fall between center and circumference, freezing the center—letting the circumference go. Another timing tie-up concerns muscular effort and facial expression. In the *Celebration* trio, I clicked at the instant when muscular effort to reach the elevation had been spent and momentary relaxation conveys triumph rather than strain. If I had wanted an expression of frenzy I would have shot earlier and faster—at the moment of greatest stress.

Lighting and timing must also be combined with tonal space, which sustains and gives architectural finality to the communication of bodily movement as in the torso composition from *Ekstasis*. If illuminated backgrounds can set the figure free in space, restricted light can embed the figure and attach it to the darkness like a sculptural relief, as in the final shot from *Deep Song*. Empty space is never empty but continually exerts dynamic influence. A light colored zone may act as a vacuum to suck the figure forward, while a dense shadow may seem to compress the figure. Tonal space orchestrated with timed lighting becomes a photographic substitute for music, enveloping, underscoring, restraining and presaging shift of mood. While the picture area is the theatre of photographic dance action, light has the most positive role, and controls the final dramatic statement. The concentrated lighting of *American Provincials* parallels the mordant quality of the dance; at the other extreme is the pervasive lighting of *Primitive Mysteries* expressing in light terms the dance's characteristic of elevation and suspension.

Two fundamental things are always a source of wonder and delight to the photographer of the dance: the dancer's imagination and the latent powers of light by which beauty and meaning can be expressed. The best pictures in this book are portraits of energy; energy of imagination, generating motor energy and transfixed by light energy.

Light is the most enthralling of all photographic elements, possessed of endless excitements. Light is to the photographer what movement is to the dancer, the active principle without which there can be no photograph, as without movement there can be no dance. The reaction I get from light is of energy, vibrating, responsive, impersonal, tireless, tapping the inexhaustible dynamics of the universe. This cosmic force is everybody's workaday tool. Light has a real parallel with dance, being itself a dance of frequencies.

The play of the abstract force of light, however, would be meaningless without its use in art, where human compassion confers value on life in all its strength and weakness. Rich in such sympathy, Martha Graham's theater portrays the vulnerable yet gallant human soul both in turmoil and serenity. She senses universal rhythms; and with her intuitive knowledge casts them in beautiful logic.

CHOREOGRAPHIC RECORD

I • CHRONOLOGICAL LIST OF DANCES • II • DESCRIPTION OF OUTSTANDING DANCES NOT PICTURED • III • MEMBERS OF DANCE GROUPS • IV • IMPORTANT TOURS • SPECIAL PERFORMANCES AND EVENTS

Louis Horst

In the first division, which includes all dances choreographed by Martha Graham between the years 1926 and 1941 inclusive, with the exception of those created for special occasions and not for concert performance, there has been no attempt made to evaluate the works as to their scale of importance. The third division and the photographs of Barbara Morgan assume some of that responsibility. Except where the designer is directly mentioned, all costumes were designed and executed by Miss Graham herself. Also, except where the designer of decor is listed, the dances were either performed with no stage settings, or, as in the case of *Lamentation, Adolescence* and *Deep Song,* employed a platform or bench of simple construction.

All music settings especially composed for the dance are indicated by asterisks. It will be noted that from April 18, 1926, to November 11, 1934, only ten works of a total of eighty-six had such musical settings. On the latter date Miss Graham presented her last dance created to music already written; the *Dance in Four Parts,* to a set of Preludes by George Antheil. From that time to the present day Miss Graham has not produced a single work for which the music was not especially composed. The American composers who supplied these settings were George Antheil, Henry Cowell, David Diamond, Lehman Engel, Ray Green, Louis Horst, Hunter Johnson, Norman Lloyd, Paul Nordoff, Alex North, and Wallingford Riegger

In the third division, the descriptions of important dances not pictured have in some cases drawn upon Miss Graham's own descriptive program notes, but mostly upon pertinent paragraphs in the reviews of our dance critics, notably those of John Martin and Mary Watkins. This list includes the most famous dances not pictured, and also those that marked the end of a period or the beginning of a new one.

	Title of Dance	Composer of Music	Date of Premiere	Place
1	Chorale (Martha Graham and trio)	César Franck	April 18, 1926	48th St. Theatre, N.Y.
2	Novelette (solo)	Schumann		
3	Tänze (trio)	Schubert		
4	Intermezzo (solo)	Brahms		
5	Maid With the Flaxen Hair (solo)	Debussy		
6	Arabesque (trio)	Debussy		
7	Clair de Lune (Martha Graham and trio)	Debussy		
8	Danse Languide (trio)	Scriabin		
9	Desir (solo)	Scriabin		
10	Deux Valses Sentimentales (solo)	Ravel		
11	Tanagra (solo)	Satie		
12	A Florentine Madonna (solo)	Rachmaninoff		
13	Gnossienne (trio)	Satie		
14	A Study in Lacquer (solo)	Bernheim		
15	Three Gopi Maidens (trio)	Cyril Scott		
16	Danse Rococo (solo)	Ravel		
17	Marionette Show (trio)	Eugene Goossens		
18	Gypsy Portrait (trio)	de Falla		
19	Angeli (trio)	Wolf-Ferrari	May 27, 1926	Kilbourn Hall, Rochester, N.Y.
20	Prelude from ''Alceste'' (Martha Graham and trio)	Gluck		
21	Scherzo (trio)	Mendelssohn	Nov. 28, 1926	Klaw Theatre, N.Y.
22	Baal Shem 1: Simchas Torah (Rejoicing) (Martha Graham and trio) 2: Vidui (Contrition) (solo)	Ernest Bloch		
23	The Moth (solo) ''The woman, like the white moth seeking the light, stalks the streets of Granada''	Debussy		
24	Alt-Wien (trio)	arr. by Louis Horst		
25	Three Poems of the East (solo) 1: ''On listening to a flute by moonlight'' 2: ''She like a dancer puts her broidered garments on'' 3: ''In measure, while the gnats of music whirr, the little amber-colored dancer moves''	*Louis Horst		
26	Peasant Sketches (solo) 1: Dance 2: Berceuse 3: In the Church	Rebikoff Tansman Tschaikowsky	Feb. 27, 1927	Guild Theatre, N.Y.
27	Tunisia (solo)	Poldini		
28	Lucrezia (solo) ''As Salome, Lucrezia did dance before the Pope, her father''	Debussy		

*Music composed especially for the dance.

	Title of Dance	Composer of Music	Date of Premiere	Place
29	La Cancion (solo) "The Gypsy's Song—sometimes of life—sometimes of death—always of love"	Defosse	Feb. 27, 1927	Guild Theatre, N.Y.
30	Spires (trio)	Bach	Oct. 16, 1927	Little Theatre, N.Y.
31	Madonna (solo)	Handel		
32	Fragilité (solo)	Scriabin		
33	Lugubre (trio)	Scriabin		
34	Poeme aile (solo)	Scriabin		
35	Tanzstück (trio)	Hindemith		
36	Revolt (solo)	Honegger		
37	Esquisse Antique (trio)	Inghelbrecht		
38	Ronde (trio)	Rhene-Baton		
39	Valse Noble (solo)	Ravel	April 22, 1928	
40	Trouveres (solo) 1: The Return of Spring 2: Complaint 3: A Song, Frank and Gay	Koechlin		
41	Immigrant (Solo) 1: Steerage 2: Strike	Slavenski		
42	Poems of 1917 (solo) 1: Song Behind the Lines 2: Dance of Death	Leo Ornstein		
43	Fragments (solo) 1: Tragedy 2: Comedy	*Louis Horst		
44	Resonances (solo) 1: Matins 2: Gamelon 3: Tocsin	Malipiero		
45	Dance (solo) "Strong, free, joyous action" (Nietzsche)	Honegger	Jan. 20, 1929	Booth Theatre, N.Y.
46	Three Florentine Verses (solo)	Zipoli		
47	Four Insincerities (solo) 1: Petulance 2: Remorse 3: Politeness 4: Vivacity	Prokofieff		
48	Cants Magics (solo) 1: Farewell 2: Greeting	Mompou		
49	Two Variations (solo) 1: Country Lane 2: City Street	Gretchaninoff		

	Title of Dance	Composer of Music	Date of Premiere	Place
50	Unbalanced (solo)	Harsanyi	March 3, 1929	Booth Theatre, N.Y.
51	Adolescence (solo)	Hindemith		
52	Danza (solo)	Milhaud		
53	Vision of the Apocalypse (group)	Reutter	April 14, 1929	
54	Moment Rustica (group)	Poulenc		
55	Heretic (Martha Graham and group)	Old Breton Song		
56	Sketches from the People (group) 1: Monotony 2: Supplication 3: Requiem	Julien Krein		
57	Prelude to a Dance (group)	Honegger	Jan. 8, 1930	Maxine Elliott Theatre, N.Y.
58	Two Chants (solo) 1: Futility 2: Ecstatic song	Krenek		
59	Lamentation (solo)	Kodaly		
60	Project in Movement for a Divine Comedy (Martha Graham and group)	no music		
61	Harlequinade (solo) 1: Pessimist 2: Optimist	Toch		
62	Two Primitive Canticles (solo) 1: Ave 2: Salve	Villa-Lobos	Feb. 2, 1931	Craig Theatre, N.Y.
63	Primitive Mysteries (Martha Graham and group) 1: Hymn to the Virgin 2: Crucifixus 3: Hosanna	*Louis Horst		
64	Rhapsodics (solo) (Song, Interlude and Dance)	Bela Bartok		
65	Bacchanale (Martha Graham and group)	*Wallingford Riegger		
66	Dolorosa (solo)	Villa-Lobos		
67	Dithyrambic (solo)	Aaron Copland	Dec. 6, 1931	Martin Beck Theatre, N.Y.
68	Serenade (solo)	Schoenberg		
69	Incantation (solo)	Villa-Lobos		

70	Ceremonials (Martha Graham and group)
	1: Vigil, Song of Approach.
	    Interlude—Fun Dance
	2: Song of Vengeance. Vision of Death.
	    Interlude—Fun Dance
	3: Sacred Formula
		*Lehman Engel	Feb. 28, 1932	Guild Theatre, N.Y.

71	Offering (solo)	Villa-Lobos	June 2, 1932	Lydia Mendelssohn Theatre, Ann Arbor, Mich.
72	Salutation (solo)	Carlos Chavez	Nov. 20, 1932	Guild Theatre, N.Y.
73	Dance Songs (solo) 1: Ceremonial 2: Morning Song 3: Satyric Festival Song 4: Song of Rapture	Imre Weisshaus		
74	Chorus of Youth (Companions) (group)	*Louis Horst		

	Title of Dance	Composer of Music	Date of Premiere	Place
75	Elegiac (solo)	Paul Hindemith	May 4, 1933 ↑	Guild Theatre, N.Y. ↑
76	Ekstasis (solo) Two lyric fragments	*Lehman Engel		
77	Tragic Patterns (Martha Graham and group) Three Choric Dances for an Antique Greek Tragedy 1: Chorus for Supplicants 2: Chorus for Maenads 3: Chorus for Furies	*Louis Horst	May 4, 1933	
78	Dance Prelude (solo)	Lopatnikoff	Nov. 19, 1933 ↑	
79	Frenetic Rhythms (solo) Three dances of possession	*Wallingford Riegger		
80	Transitions (solo) 1: Prologue 2: Theatre Piece No. 1—Sarabande 3: Theatre Piece No. 2—Pantomime 4: Epilogue	*Lehman Engel	Feb. 18, 1934 ↑	
81	Phantasy (solo) 1: Prelude 2: Gavotte 3: Musette	Schoenberg		
82	Four Casual Developments (trio)	Henry Cowell		
83	Celebration (group)	*Louis Horst		
84	Integrales (Martha Graham and group) Shapes of Ancestral Wonder	Edgar Varese	April 22, 1934	Alvin Theatre, N.Y.
85	Dance in Four Parts (solo) 1: Quest 2: Derision 3: Dream 4: Sportive Tragedy	George Antheil	Nov. 11, 1934 ↑	Guild Theatre, N.Y. ↑
86	American Provincials 1: Act of Piety (solo) 2: Act of Judgment (Martha Graham and group)	*Louis Horst		
87	Praeludium (solo)	*Paul Nordoff	Feb. 10, 1935 ↑	
88	Course (Martha Graham and group)	*George Antheil		
89	Frontier (solo) An American Perspective of the Plains	*Louis Horst Decor by Isamu Noguchi	April 28, 1935 ↑	
90	Marching Song (Martha Graham and trio)	*Lehman Engel		
91	Panorama (Martha Graham and group) 1: Theme of Dedication 2: Imperial Theme 3: Popular Theme	*Norman Lloyd Setting by Arch Lauterer	Aug. 14, 1935	Bennington, Vt.
92	Formal Dance (solo)	*David Diamond	Nov. 10, 1935 ↑	Guild Theatre, N.Y. ↑
93	Imperial Gesture (solo)	*Lehman Engel		
94	Horizons (Martha Graham and group) 1: Migration (New Trails) 2: Dominion (Sanctified Power) 3: Building Motif (Homesteading) 4: Dance of Rejoicing	*Louis Horst Decor by Alexander Calder	Feb. 23, 1936	

	Title of Dance	Composer of Music	Date of Premiere	Place

95	Chronicle (Martha Graham and group)
	1: Dances Before Catastrophe
	   (a) Spectre—1914 (Drums—Red Shroud—Lament)
	   (b) Masque (Idolatry of Tradition)
	2: Dances After Catastrophe
	   (a) Steps in the Street (Devastation—Exile)
	   (b) Tragic Holiday (In Memoriam)
	3: Prelude to Action (Unity—Pledge to the Future)
		*Wallingford Riegger
		Decor by Isamu Noguchi
			Dec. 20, 1936	Guild Theatre, N.Y.

96	Opening Dance (solo)	*Norman Lloyd	July 30, 1937	Bennington, Vt.
97	Immediate Tragedy (solo)	*Henry Cowell		
98	Deep Song (solo)	*Henry Cowell	Dec. 19, 1937	Guild Theatre, N.Y.
99	American Lyric (Martha Graham and group)	*Alex North	Dec. 26, 1937	
100	American Document (Martha Graham and group)	*Ray Green Costumes by Martha Graham	Aug. 6, 1938	Bennington, Vt.
101	Columbiad (solo)	*Louis Horst Decor by Philip Stapp Costumes by Edythe Gilfond	Dec. 27, 1939	St. James Theatre, N.Y.

102	"Every Soul is a Circus..." (Martha Graham and group)
	"Every Soul is a circus
	  Every mind is a tent
	  Every heart is a sawdust ring
	  Where the circling race is spent"—Vachel Lindsay
		*Paul Nordoff
		Setting by Philip Stapp
		Costumes by Martha Graham		

103	El Penitente (Martha Graham and two men)	*Louis Horst Setting by Arch Lauterer Costumes by Martha Graham	Aug. 11, 1940	Bennington, Vt.
104	Letter to the World (Martha and group)	*Hunter Johnson Setting by Arch Lauterer Costumes by Edythe Gilfond		

II • IMPORTANT TOURS • SPECIAL PERFORMANCES AND EVENTS

April 26, 27, 28, 1929. Manhattan Opera House, New York ... Danced principal role (with Charles Weidman) in Richard Strauss' "Ein Heldenleben," presented by the Neighborhood Playhouse under the direction of Irene Lewisohn with the Cleveland Symphony Orchestra, Nikolai Sokoloff conducting.

Feb. 20, 21, 22, 1930. Mecca Auditorium, New York ... Danced principal role (with Charles Weidman) in Charles Martin Loeffler's "A Pagan Poem," presented by the Neighborhood Playhouse under the direction of Irene Lewisohn with the Cleveland Symphony Orchestra, Nikolai Sokoloff conducting.

April 11, 12 and 14, 1930. Metropolitan Opera House, Philadelphia, Pa. and April 22 and 23, 1930. Metropolitan Opera House, New York ... Danced principal role (The Chosen One) in Igor Stravinsky's "Le Sacre du Printemps," with the Philadelphia Symphony Orchestra, Leopold Stokowski conducting.

Appeared with Blanche Yurka in Sophocles' "Electra" at Ann Arbor Dramatic Festival. Week of May 25, 1931, and on tour.

Was granted the first Fellowship to a dancer by the John Simon Guggenheim Memorial Foundation, March, 1932.

Appeared with her group on Inaugural Program of Radio City Music Hall (Rockefeller Center, New York City), Dec. 27, 1932.

Assisted Katherine Cornell and Guthrie McClintic in the production of Andre Obey's "Lucrece," Belasco Theatre, New York. Jan., 1933.

Produced Six Miracle Plays for Stage Alliance at Guild Theatre, New York. Feb. 5 and 12, 1933.

Directed dances for Katherine Cornell's production of "Romeo and Juliet." Nov., 1934.

Appointed by Mayor La Guardia to New York Municipal Art Committee. Jan., 1935.

Directed the Movement for Archibald Macleish's play "Panic," Imperial Theatre, New York. March 14 and 15, 1935.

March 15 to April 28, 1936. First trans-continental tour in solo recitals ... Cranbrook, Mich. • Detroit, Mich. • Seattle, Wash. • Portland, Ore. • Tacoma, Wash. • Oakland, Cal. • Carmel, Cal. • San Francisco, Cal. • San Jose, Cal. • Palo Alto, Cal. • Santa Barbara, Cal. • Los Angeles, Cal. • Colorado Springs, Colo. • Chicago, Ill. • Oxford, Ohio.

Danced for President and Mrs. Roosevelt at The White House, Feb. 26, 1937.

March 12 to May 2, 1937. Second trans-continental tour with company of 15 ... Madison, Wis. • Chicago, Ill. • Billings, Mont. • Vancouver, B.C. • Tacoma, Wash. • Seattle, Wash, • San Francisco, Cal. • Carmel, Cal. • Santa Barbara, Cal. • Los Angeles, Cal. • Tallahassee, Fla. • Lynchburg, Va. • Pittsburgh, Pa. • New York, N.Y.

May, 1, 1938. Produced group dance for New York World's Fair Pre-view Pageant.

Feb. 23 to March 23, 1939. Third trans-continental tour with company of 17 ... Bryn Mawr, Pa. • Atlanta, Ga. • Montgomery, Ala. • Memphis, Tenn. • Denton, Texas • Tucson, Ariz. • Los Angeles, Cal. • Santa Barbara, Cal. • San Francisco, Cal. • Provo, U. • Kansas City, Mo. • Chicago, Ill. • Milwaukee, Wis. • Ithaca, N.Y.

April 30, 1939. Staged group dance "Tribute to Peace" for Opening Day Ceremonies of New York World's Fair.

Feb. 12 to April 5, 1940. Fourth trans-continental tour with company of 15 ... Philadelphia, Pa. • Atlantic City, N.J. • Richmond Va. • Charleston, S.C. • Baton Rouge, La. • Austin, Tex. • Forth Worth, Tex. • Dallas, Tex. • Phoenix, Ariz. • Los Angeles, Cal. • Santa Barbara, Cal. • San Francisco, Cal. • Eugene, Ore. • Seattle, Wash. • Corvallis, Ore. • Hiram, Ohio. • Plattsburg, N.Y. • New York, N.Y. • Hartford, Conn. • Mansfield, Pa.

Signed with WGN Concert Bureau for trans-continental tour 1941-42.

III • DESCRIPTION OF OUTSTANDING DANCES NOT PICTURED

8 DANSE LANGUIDE • The first dance Martha Graham created for any dancer other than herself. It was a trio designed to use movement as a medium for group composition rather than a literary concept.

9 DESIR • This solo was the first dance evolved from an inner compulsion. It is only important as it marks a turning towards a newer expressional medium.

10 DEUX VALSES SENTIMENTALES • A sidelong, rather conscious glance at sentimentality, as epitomized in a waltz. Miss Graham's first satire.

11 TANAGRA • An expression of a classical figure. Performed with an effective use of draperies, it was the last dance still showing a definite influence of Denishawn background.

32 FRAGILITÉ • A portrayal of the fragile qualities of romantic womanhood. It was done in a stylized transparent evening dress made of organdy.

36 REVOLT • The first composition expressing a conscious awareness of the changing social scene which reflected the today of that day.

41 IMMIGRANT (Steerage—Strike) • Two studies changing from the alternating pious fatalism and gay abandon of the ''steerage'' to the jeering animalistic defiance of immigrant labor alive to new forces and broader visions, fighting through ''strike'' to achieve them.

42 POEMS OF 1917 (Song Behind the Lines. Dance of Death) • War-mad motherhood in a lullaby of empty arms; a bitter cry against the useless conventions of war.

43 FRAGMENTS (Tragedy—Comedy) • Based upon the ideals of the old Greek theatre, but common to all theatre. Beneath Tragedy's robe lurks the vividness of Comedy's garment. This dance was the first for which the music was written after the dance was completed. The music (by Louis Horst) was for flute and gong.

47 FOUR INSINCERITIES • Malignant and impudent comment on four commonplace human qualities; a satirical burlesque of a few of our weaknesses.

51 ADOLESCENCE • A projection of the mental and emotional processes, the uncertainties, the yearnings and the shyness of the difficult age. Youth, curious, fearful, swept by strange visions and dreams.

53 VISION OF THE APOCALYPSE • A theme and variations based upon the following quotation: ''And he being of pure thought and young and right earnest, did fast and pray. And there was granted unto him a vision like unto that of John, the saint, in the holy book of Revelations. And that same vision was of the woes of man and the burden of his sins, and the young monk, being right gentle and pure of thought, stood distressed thereat and bowed down.''
The variations deal with Vision, Toil, Famine, Blasphemy, Ruthlessness, Pestilence, Mourning, Prayer and Death. It is Miss Graham's first presentation of a work for a large group.

55 HERETIC • The action outlines the stiff-necked, merciless cruelty and oppression of intolerance against a figure pleading for tolerance. Stark, elemental tragedy presented with a taut economy of means. The music (an old Breton song) consists of only eleven measures played over and over.

60 PROJECT IN MOVEMENT FOR A DIVINE COMEDY • Notable chiefly as being the first adventure of Miss Graham in the field of dancing without music. ''It is a heroic concept for soloist and ensemble cast in the mold of hypothetical Blake illustrations for Dante, and is strikingly of the theatre.'' (John Martin.)

67 DITHYRAMBIC • A solo dance of large scope, lasting thirteen minutes. A barbaric crescendo expressing the dionysiac passion of the ancient dithyramb. A series of ecstatic variations on a ritualistic theme, performed to the hard, granite-like *Piano Variations* by Aaron Copland.

70 CEREMONIALS • A long work cast in the primitive idiom and based on some of the sacred ceremonial formulas of our American Indians. A cycle of spiritual experiences.

79 FRENETIC RHYTHMS • Three dances that ''present the daemons of possession in various guises, such as atavism (grotesque animality), introspection (pseudo-Oriental autointoxication), and extraversion (arrant vulgarity); all treated as devils to be exorcised.'' (John Martin.)

88 COURSE • A group dance based upon a running theme. It is the energy of youth stated in dance movement reminiscent of the motor activities of sport; running, leaping, jumping and the suspension of rest.

91 PANORAMA • The first Workshop Production of the Bennington School of the Dance, Panorama endeavors to present three themes which are basically American. Theme of Dedication is based on that early intensity of fanaticism with which our Puritan fathers sang their hymn of dedication of a new world. Imperial Theme chooses a southern locale where was to be found the most striking expression of a people in bondage ridden by superstitions and strange fears. Popular Theme is of the people and their awakening social consciousness in the contemporary scene.

94 HORIZONS • A cycle based on the theme of Exploration and Discovery. While not specifically American the dances were built on themes abstracted from the American background. An innovation was the employment of Alexander Calder's Mobiles as moving decor, a new conscious use of space. They were presented as visual preludes to the dances to enlarge the sense of horizon.

95 CHRONICLE • Chronicle traces the ugly logic of imperialism, the need for conquest, the inevitability of the conflict, the unavoidable unmasking of the rooted evil, and the approach of the masses to a logical conclusion. It shows the brutalization of conquest, the hyprocrisy of imperialism, the marching of men without cause, without direction, masking of the memory of conflict with memorials and the taut gathering of new energies and new forces.

IV • MEMBERS OF DANCE GROUPS (1926-1941)

GIRLS

Alvarez, Anita (1934-1939)

Babitz, Thelma (1936-1939)

Biracree, Thelma (1926)

Bird, Bonnie (1933-1937)

Bird, Dorothy (1931-1937)

Brenner, Sydney (1931-1933)

Briton, Virginia (1929-1931)

Bunsick, Hortense (1929-1931)

*Butler, Ethel (1933-   )

Cornell, Grace (1931)

Creston, Louise (1929-1934)

*Dudley, Jane (1935-   )

Emery, Irene (1929-1930)

*Erdman, Jean (1938-   )

*Fisher, Nelle (1937-   )

*Flier, Frieda (1936-   )

*Fonaroff, Nina (1937-   )

Gerson, Beatrice (1931-1932)

Gilmour, Ailes (1930-1933)

Haim, Mattie (1931-1934)

*Halpern, Elizabeth (1939-   )

Harris, Natalie (1937-1939)

Hill, Martha (1930-1931)

Liandre, Lil (1934-1936)

Macdonald, Betty (1926-1930)

Marchowsky, Marie (1934-1940)

*Maslow, Sophie (1931-   )

*Mazia, Marjorie (1936-   )

*Personnel of Company as of 1941

Mehlman, Lily (1931-1936)

Nadler, Freema (1931-1932)

Nelson, Pauline (1931-1933)

O'Donnell, May (1932-1938)

Radin, Mary (1932-1934)

Ray, Lillian (1929-1934)

Reese, Kitty (1929-1930)

Rivoire, Mary (1929-1933)

Rosenstein, Sylvia (1929)

Rudy, Ethel (1929-1934)

Sabin, Evelyn (1926-1930)

Savelli, Rosina (1926-1930)

Schneider, Florence (1934-1936)

Schoenberg, Bessie (1930-1931)

Selby, Catherine (1932)

Shapero, Lillian (1929-1934)

Shurr, Gertrude (1930-1938)

Slagle, Kathleen (1935-1938)

Sokolow, Anna (1930-1938)

Wasserstrom, Sylvia (1929-1930)

White, Ruth (1929-1932)

Woodruff, Joan (1930-1933)

MEN

*Campbell, David (1940-   )

*Cunningham, Merce (1939-   )

Hall, George (1940)

*Hawkins, Erick (1938-   )

Stevens, Jr., Housely (1938-1940)

*Zellmer, David (1940-   )

	Title of Dance	*Composer of Music*	*Date of Premiere*	*Place*
114	Punch and the Judy	Robert McBride	August 10, 1941	College Theatre, Bennington, Vt.
115	Land Be Bright	Arthur Krentz	March 14, 1942	Chicago Civic Opera House, Chicago, Ill.
116	Salem Shore	Paul Nordoff	December 26, 1943	46th Street Theatre, NYC
117	Deaths and Entrances	Hunter Johnson		
118	Imagined Wing (Jeux du Printemps)	Darius Milhaud	December 30, 1944	Library of Congress, Washington, D.C.
119	Herodiade	Paul Hindemith		
120	Appalachian Spring	Aaron Copland		
121	Dark Meadow	Carlos Chavez	January 23, 1946	Plymouth Theatre, NYC
122	Cave of the Heart	Samuel Barber	May 10, 1946	McMillan Theatre, Columbia University, NYC
123	Errand Into the Maze	Gian-Carlo Menotti	February 28, 1947	Ziegfeld Theatre, NYC
124	Night Journey	William Schuman	May 3, 1947	Cambridge High School, Cambridge, Mass.
125	Diversion of Angels	Norman Dello Joio	August 13, 1948	Palmer Auditorium, New London, Conn.
126	Judith	William Schuman	January 4, 1950	Columbia Auditorium, Louisville, Ky.
127	Eye of Anguish	Vincent Persichetti	January 22, 1950	46th Street Theatre, NYC
128	Gospel of Eve	Paul Nordoff		
129	The Triumph of Saint Joan	Norman Dello Joio	December 5, 1951	Columbia Auditorium, Louisville, Ky.
130	Canticle for Innocent Comedians	Thomas Ribbink	April 22, 1952	Juilliard School of Music, NYC
131	Voyage	William Schuman	May 27, 1953	Alvin Theatre, NYC
132	Ardent Song	Alan Hovhaness	March 18, 1954	Saville Theatre, London
133	Seraphic Dialogue	Norman Dello Joio	May 8, 1955	ANTA Theatre, NYC
134	Clytemnestra	Halim El-Dabh	April 1, 1958	Adelphi Theatre, NYC
135	Embattled Garden	Carlos Surinach	April 3, 1958	Adelphi Theatre, NYC
136	Episodes: Part I	Anton Webern (Passacaglia Op. 1/Six Pieces for Orchestra Op. 6)	May 14, 1959	City Center, NYC

	Title of Dance	Composer of Music	Date of Premiere	Place
137	Acrobats of God	Carlos Surinach	April 27, 1960	54th Street Theatre, NYC
138	Alcestis	Vivian Fine	April 29, 1960	54th Street Theatre, NYC
139	Visionary Recital	Robert Starer	April 16, 1961	54th Street Theatre, NYC
140	One More Gaudy Night	Halim El-Dabh	April 20, 1961	54th Street Theatre, NYC
141	Phaedra	Robert Starer	March 4, 1962	Broadway Theatre, NYC
142	A Look at Lightning	Halim El-Dabh	March 5, 1962	Broadway Theatre, NYC
143	Secular Games	Robert Starer (Concerto a Tre)	August 17, 1962	Palmer Auditorium, New London, Conn.
144	Legend of Judith	Mordecai Seter	October 25, 1962	Habima Theatre, Tel Aviv, Israel
145	Circe	Alan Hovhaness	September 6, 1963	Prince of Wales Theatre, London
146	The Witch of Endor	William Schuman	November 2, 1965	54th Street Theatre, NYC
147	Part Real-Part Dream	Mordecai Seter	November 3, 1965	54th Street Theatre, NYC
148	Cortege of Eagles	Eugene Lester	February 21, 1967	Mark Hellinger Theatre, NYC
149	Dancing Ground	Ned Rorem (Eleven Studies for Eleven Players)	February 24, 1967	Mark Hellinger Theatre, NYC
150	A Time of Snow	Norman Dello Joio	May 25, 1968	George Abbott Theatre, NYC
151	Plain of Prayer	Eugene Lester	May 29, 1968	George Abbott Theatre, NYC
152	The Lady of The House of Sleep	Robert Starer	May 30, 1968	George Abbott Theatre, NYC
153	The Archaic Hours	Eugene Lester	April 11, 1969	New York City Center, NYC
154	Mendicants of Evening	David Walker	May 2, 1973	Alvin Theatre, NYC
155	Myth of a Voyage	Alan Hovhaness	May 3, 1973	Alvin Theatre, NYC
156	Holy Jungle	Robert Starer	April 1974	Mark Hellinger Theatre, NYC
157	Jacob's Dream	Mordecai Seter	July 1974	Jerusalem, Israel
158	Lucifer	Halim El-Dabh	June 19, 1975	Uris Theatre, NYC
159	Adorations	Classical Guitar	December 8, 1975	Mark Hellinger Theatre, NYC

	Title of Dance	Composer of Music	Date of Premiere	Place
160	Point of Crossing	Mordecai Seter		
161	The Scarlet Letter	Hunter Johnson	December 22, 1975	Mark Hellinger Theatre, NYC
162	O Thou Desire Who Art About To Sing	Meyer Kupferman (Fantasy for Violin and Piano)	May 17, 1977	Lunt-Fontanne Theatre, NYC
163	Shadows	Gian-Carlo Menotti (Cantilena e Scherzo)	May 24, 1977	Lunt-Fontanne Theatre, NYC
164	The Owl and the Pussycat	Carlos Surinach	June 26, 1978	Metropolitan Opera House, NYC
165	Ecuatorial	Edgard Varèse (Ecuatorial)	June 27, 1978	Metropolitan Opera House, NYC
166	Flute of Pan	Traditional		
167	Frescoes	Samuel Barber (Two Arias from "Antony and Cleopatra")	December 9, 1978	Metropolitan Museum of Art, NYC
168	Revival and Reworking of "Episodes"	Anton Webern	July 24, 1979	Convent Garden, London
169	Judith (Reworking)	Edgard Varèse	April 29, 1980	Metropolitan Opera House, NYC

*Chronological listing of dances from 1941-1980 provided courtesy of the Martha Graham Center.

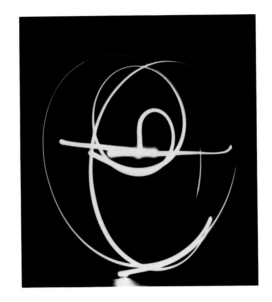

LIGHT SIGNATURE